Playing the Word

Books by Dan Jaffe

Dan Freeman
Frontier Literature: Images of the American West (ed. with John Knoepfle)
The First Tuesday in November
Kansas City Outloud (ed.)
For Kids by Kids (ed. with Sylvia Griffith Wheeler)
The Muscles and the Bones That Carry Us to Love
All Cats Turn Gray When the Sun Goes Down, a jazz opera
Seasons of the River
Round for One Voice
Kansas City Outloud II (ed.)
Festival
Playing the Word

Playing the Word

Jazz Poems

by

Dan Jaffe

BkMk Press
University of Missouri-Kansas City

BkMk Press
University of Missouri-Kansas City
5101 Rockhill Road
Kansas City, Missouri 64110
(816) 235-2558 (voice)
(816) 235-2611 (fax)
http://www.umkc.edu/bkmk/
bkmk@umkc.edu

BkMk Press receives financial assistance from the Missouri Arts Council, a state agency.

Cover photo, Thelonious Monk, New York City, 1949
Cover photo and centerfold (pp. 36-37) Copyright © Herman Leonard
"Bopping at Minton's" (p. 67) Design, Tamar Jaffe
Photo of Charlie Parker's gravesite (p. 77) Copyright © Allene Mahogany
The Players (pp. 78-79) compiled by Kevin Rabas

Cover and book design, Thomas Zvi Wilson

Library of Congress Cataloging-in-Publication Data

Jaffe, Dan.
     Playing the word: Jazz poems / Dan Jaffe.
          p. cm.
     ISBN 1-886157-34-0
     1. Jazz--Poetry. 2. Jazz musicians--Poetry. I. Title.
     PS3560.A3 P55 2001
     811'.54--dc21

                                                  2001043418

To the Players

In memory of George Salisbury

Acknowledgments

The Mid-America Poetry Review, the *Kansas City Star*, *New Letters*, the *New York Times*, *Dacotah Territory 13* (Moorehead State University.), *Stiletto II* (Howling Dog Press), *Round for One Voice* (University of Arkansas Press), *Kansas City Outloud* (BkMk Press of UMKC), *The Missouri Poets* (Eads Bridge Press: St. Louis University), *Voices From the Interior* (BkMk Press).

"Blues for Bernice Six" was part of a concert chorale, *A Lesson In Geography*, performed under the auspices of the National Endowment for the Arts and the Mid-America Arts Alliance.

"If This Were Eden," "All Cats Turn Gray When the Sun Goes Down," and "Gravedigger Blues," were parts of *All Cats Turn Gray When the Sun Goes Down*, a jazz opera performed at different times under the auspices of the University of Missouri-Kansas City Conservatory of Music; The Nelson Gallery of Art, and the Henry Street Theatre (New York City), also, under the title *Without Memorial Banners*, at the Music Teachers National Association convention.

"For Herman Leonard, Photographer" was part of a show at the New World School of the Arts, Miami, Florida.

"Play On" was written for George Salisbury Day as proclaimed by the governor of Missouri and the mayor of Kansas City, Missouri. It was performed on that day at a concert at UMKC. Many of the other poems in this book have also been performed at George Salisbury Memorial concerts at UMKC.

"Bop Talk," "Play On," "Listening," "But Anyhow," "Over on Main," "Poem for Two Pianos," and "Unveiling the Bird, Lincoln Cemetery, Kansas City, Missouri," were a part of the gallery show and concert at the Barstow School, Kansas City, Missouri. They are now part of a permanent display at the Phoenix Jazz Bar in the Ameristar Casino, Kansas City, Missouri.

My thanks go to Robert Stewart for candid and illuminating editing and to Thomas Zvi Wilson for unwavering support and help.

A special note of appreciation to Herman Leonard for the inspiration of his work and the opportunity to use his photographs. Thanks also to Jenny Bagart of the Leonard Studio for her cooperation.

I am especially grateful to Barbara Gillman, who provided unceasing encouragement and assistance to make this a better and more successful book. "Playing the word" was the phrase Nicole Yarling used when Dan Jaffe appeared with her group. Barbara Gillman sugested it be used as this book's title.

Listening for the Jazz Poem

In 1962 I read poems as part of a poetry and jazz program in Kansas City. We didn't perform the poems and music together, but everything was coordinated by mood and tempo. The musicians were extraordinary. George Salisbury, the great Kansas City piano player, protégé of Mary Lou Williams, headed up a group of Milt Abel, Vince Bilardo, Arch Martin, and Dick Busey.

Poetry and jazz do go together. I found it easy and natural. Over four decades of performing with jazz musicians, I've learned that jazz helps an audience listen more closely to poems, and poems can open an audience to meanings in music. Poetry and jazz programs also enlarge the audience. They bring music and writing people together in a way that is too rare.

I became a jazz fan when I was 12 years old. Uncle Phil Jaffe, the family hero just back from World War II, took me and my younger cousin Larry to a concert at the Adams Theater in Newark, New Jersey. Louie Prima and Lionel Hampton cooked, and I was hooked. So began my life of searching for jazz.

I had already begun to fiddle with poems, but I had no notion of how my love for poetry and jazz would affect each other. At first I responded to certain similarities. Jazz and poetry were both rhythmical, driven by sound and emphasis. In both, feeling sizzled. I knew they were brothers right away. But those first poems I read were not jazz poems just because I read them in a jazz situation.

Over the years, I've come to wonder if my love for jazz grew as it did because I admired the musicians so much. Few of the people I've met in my life have seemed so authentic. Their music moves me as few things can.

The players and their music have become almost indistinguishable for me. I think of my friend Herb Six's definition of jazz, not technical at all, great philosophy put so simply. Herb Six, jazz piano player, composer, teacher of jazz greats, put it this way: "Jazz," he said, "that's what jazz musicians play."

It reminds me of Robert Frost talking about "the reality of the indefinable," only more colloquial. Defining the jazz poem is about as possible as explaining the mysteries. All I can do is point to the deeper paradoxes of art.

Let's assume the jazz poem must first be a poem. It must somehow fulfill its form as a poem, but it better swing whether you can identify its form or not. It needs to surprise us the way jazz does.

Whatever else you say, add history and pain, jazz players, the immediacy of a situation, the spontaneity of creation and the great instrumental skill required to the equation. Add "chops" and "soul." Or better yet, listen to "Ornithology."

Sure, the jazz poem must first be a poem. And it must be related to jazz. But how? The easiest connection is subject matter. Often it's about the jazz world, about the joints and players, the music itself, associated incidents and accidents. But that is not enough. Poems are often not about what they seem to be about. They talk about one thing in terms of another. What's at the heart of the poem, as with jazz, is not what you can paraphrase. Soul ain't sentimentality. Gwendolyn Brooks's "We Real Cool" talks about pool players and early death. But its jazz rhythms and its blues overtones make its words mean more. It is certainly a jazz poem. Would a subject-matter label identify it as such? Not likely.

We've got to get to the music, to the way the music of the poem and the music we call jazz come together. The jazz poem in its stops and starts, in the click of its fricatives and the lushness of its vowels must connect us to what the players and the vocalists of jazz create, to jazz itself and how it feels and sounds.

The poem may strike us because of its swing or the use of the musician's vocabulary or some subtle observation only someone who really knows jazz would make; but the main question is whether the poem is true to the jazz experience, whether it really suggests the music. Is it outside or inside? It's not enough that it be about jazz. It must be jazz. This is not a matter of credentials. A jazz musician might attempt to write a poem about a gig and fail, just as a trumpet player might attempt to play with soul and somehow fail.

These are objectives. We may or may not fulfill them. We go to our graves trying.

— D.J.

Playing the Word

I   in the Celestial City

High Flyers

I'm listening to "Ornithology"
as two brown pelicans wheel by the corner
of my balcony
in swooping counterpoint
to Bird's quick notes.

Those high flyers
make me think of you, Martin,
your words rising from the mountain:
the open flow of your phrasing, those
buoyant chords that pull us toward you,
the heartbeat that charges the silence.

Bird did it, too.
He told the story with his horn.
He broke through the closed doors of the spirit.
He bopped down the walls. His
swinging blues let loose the soul.

So I know, now,
you're on the bandstand with Bird,
holding your conversations
in be-bop time,
your spirals of notes
unwinding from the corners of the world
as we spin free.

Over on Main

Joe Donassi dreamed he wore Sinatra's shoes,
shining like bottles behind the register.
It helped that he could pass
for a young Old Blue Eyes.
It was his profile, the way he
curled his collar back,
turned up his sleeves. Somebody would say,
"Frankie!" surprised he could be there.

Sure, Joe couldn't sing a note.
But floating behind a bar transformed him
into a character for a film in tough town,
who always had a girl about to drop by
and looked like he could tell you
whatever you needed to find out.

But it wasn't enough, Joe knew, nohow.
Not without the music.
So he opened a joint over on Main,
two doors from the deli, and he got George,
George Salisbury, who never said nothing, never,
who just played till nobody in the joint said anything, either.
They just listened, not even the drinks pouring,
to those lit notes that shattered the shadows.
Not even Joe Donassi
worried about Frankie then.

Listening

for Milt Abel

What blows out of the streets
almost blows him out of his mind.
There's no number to call
that will make peace,
& he's given up
on answers. Even the spire
of the cathedral
sticks in his ribs
as he hunts for himself.

What can he do but lay his hands
on wisps of smoke, curls of air?
Of these, of notes and words,
of the shine of a polished brass,
he makes longitudes and lattitudes.

What rumbles out of his chest
like memories loosed into ether?
A flap and a flutter of gulls' wings,
notes like names rising,
a geneology that makes the player pure,
a music that washes the world
with feeling and cries out,
Lord Lord!

We listen,
curling back into ourselves
like a bass player's hands
feeling currents of light
in the blood.

Turning the Town

Pendergast's just a wide open memory;
Harry, a haberdasher turned myth,
but Basie's tunes keep right on turning the town
from 18th and Vine to the Bottoms.
Yah, they say, cruising the Plaza, searching
for jazz down by the river, Yah, they say.
This is still Bird's town,
still Jimmy Rushing's town.
It ain't a Pub Crawl. It's a demonstration.

In Kansas City you can mesh flesh
With Claude "Fiddler" Williams, with Jay McShann.
Hell, all these years
they've been paying
your dues with their tunes.
A big wind scats through Kansas City.
You never know who's jazzing it up.

Down on Central,
smelling distance from the river,
an old Buick pulls up in front of the Phoenix.
Speedy Higgins is on the bandstand, with Rusty Tucker,
Speedy in a purple sport shirt
from a jazz cruise out of Miami
when he was just a kid of 75.
The snow ain't here yet, but Speedy's cool.
He makes much of the blues,
Of Kaaaaaaan sas   Ciiiiiii ty.
He stretches time out, stretches it
over the years,   slow   it   seems,   so slow   sometimes,
but no matter   somehow   always   swinging.

It's the beat
keeps them going
the blues beat,
that Kansas City beat,
the blues in the bop beat
keeps them shaking,
their heads bobbing
to the beat
never missing a word but
clapping for the alto
lowering shrill voices
for the bass.

Through the plate glass
Speedy sees the Buick pull up,
Ricky Anderson's bass poking out the back window.
We're all waiting
for Lonnie McFadden or Rod Fleeman,
for What's His Name
who blew us away last week.

The town keeps changing,
but it's always Basie's town,
always Bird's town,
and that new cat,
his fur hardly singed. Man,
he can blow.
He stood up there and they all
took off their socks at once,
'cause this town
belongs to the players.

For Albert Verweire, Musician
1924-1970

Behind a college concert hall,
Its parking lot empty but for us,
With roses, carnations, and lavender mums,
With a scented flute of flowers,
An overlay of petals
Covering a spare snow tire
And a rusted jack,
We came in three cars,
But we leave in one,
Carting also a bass, a fifth,
And a roadmap to a graveyard
Halfway across a state famous for silences.

We drive into dawn,
Each telling each
Stories to name his life,
Numbly heading into Springfield.
All the way a windy rain:
Something to do with highs and lows
The weatherman says,
But probably just for spite,
To keep us worried or late.
We remark on a roadside willow,
Its branches almost knotted
Like a woman's hair.

If you were here, Al,
You'd whisper us closer
Or simply smile some good into our anger.
Right now George feels tighter than an F sharp,

And Cleo says you'd surely approve
A taste for the occasion,
Something to come in on.
We all buy mints for our breath,
For your family's sake.

Later, after the college orchestra,
After your best student's flute
And your best friend's Bach,
All restraint,
Like a holding back of tears;
For all of us
And for himself most,
George will blow you out
To your own jazz.

But even that's somehow not enough.
Not for George who cries so hard afterwards
He can't find his coat sleeves with his arms,
Nor for any in the wet audience
At the military graveyard.
And I know now, Al,
Taps is a dull dirty tune
Unless you jazz it up.

Play On

God saves the world some say
for the sake of a few holy men.
For their sake He keeps the garden.
On nights empty even of stars
you may hear their voices
on the wind, their melodies
woven in the currents of the river.
Round about midnight we know
it's true. We know Monk runs deep,
that Bird lives in pure sound
that Mingus still plucks a spectral bass,
that Hotlips never put down his horn,
that those puffs of cloud over the Missouri
are a line of notes,
that the planet dances through the heavens
because somewhere somebody's blowing a riff.
They play/they played/they are playing—
All the great ones who linger
always at the edge of consciousness:
Emily and Walt
and serious Percy Bysshe
who in a different lingo
played the Adonais Blues,
Lady and Max and Satch,
and Langston Hughes,
and Mary Lou in the Celestial City
which is always here
so long as Bechet or McShann,
Bassie or Dizzy,
or George Salisbury of Lawrence, Kansas,
play not just for the fanfare,
the flowers or the fame,
but for the music
that keeps us going.
So we listen together
for what drives the world.
Play, George, play; play on, play on.

II   hanging out

Notes from the Williamsburg

after Sonny Rollins

The breeze is up,
almost a gust,
and you're up, too,
hanging out with yourself
at 3 a.m., the city
down below, currents of air
swirling into jazz.
The riff you play from the bridge
floats back in the wash of night,
vibrating off the struts.
                               Yah,
you say to the low tones,
give me these high places,
so the soul can soar.

Each night's different,
each dawn, each tune,
each time. You never know
where you're going
till the music takes you.
And then it's done gone
with friends who pass
into the mist. Somehow
they're both still there
suspended in ether,
framed in the arch of memory,
a parable of notes
that curl from the mouth of the horn.

After Hours

Lights out at Birdland
we cruised up to Harlem,
to 125th and Lenox Ave,
catching the lights just right.
There we stumbled down hard stairs
under Fatima's Turkish Bath neon,
at 4 a.m. two white boys
thinking nothing of it
thinking jazz thinking Hot Lips
will get us in and he did
and we sauntered by the black cop
leaning next to the shaky card table outside the door.
We were Hot Lips' boys he told them.
Don't be fooled by what you see.

From bandstands downtown they drifted in,
drummers and horn players,
cause they couldn't sleep or needed a drink
or breakfast or just because
of habit or Hot Lips or the big blonde,
her exuberant hair piled high
floating like a beacon behind the bar.

We drank beer or bourbon,
whatever somebody bought.
Whispers in the murky light, a hand
on the shoulder telling us something
we hadn't earned, pure gifts
'cause we were there.

Later they turned up the lights
and served up coffee and steaming eggs.
Afterward we hobbled out and up
those metal-tipped stairs to the car
and morning and the bright ride back
to Jersey, all the way the roaring sun
beating against our brains.

Jazz Joint, NYC

It's hard to find an empty chair
through streaks of smoke that autograph
the air. In a blue-lit mirror, a match
lights up a face sketched in despair.

The rhythm section's tempos fill
the room; two towering trumpets
spill sharp notes into the dark.
The alto blurts its own free will.

The joint is full of knowing eyes
flickering to the beat. Someone
cries, "Kiss me, Baby, no more
lies." The music almost sighs.

Bass Talk

for Ron Roberts

Ron's feet hurt
from treks he took
and meant to take,
but now he'd rather
sit than lumber
down a trail,
"Any trail," he says.
For thirty years
he hauled a bass
up and down stairs
in and out of joints,
till he gave it up
to play guitar.
Why hold up a melody
with jagged chords
when you can play it
and weave your way
between the trees
along the creek bed?
"I'm up front with guitar,"
he says. "It's all mine,
even if that old bass
calls me back sometimes.
It must be all that pain
walking the Trail of Tears."
"Hell, you don't look
Cherokee to me," I say.
"Well, Superman," says he,
"vision ain't your instrument.
But that don't matter.
Sioux or Cherokee,
Beaver or Gator,
it's all the same.
My tribe's Musician.
I joined the nation
on the bandstand."

Poem for Two Pianos

Marian and Ahmad chat across the keys,
leaning forward,
testing their words,
knowing what they say
means less than they want
to say, knowing,
there are ways of meaning more
by saying less.

They pause,
conscious of the silence
and their tensed fingers.
"I will be absolutely shameless,"
says Marian, "and ask
if we can do something together."
So they play "You Do Something to Me"
each his own way
but always, somehow, still together.

For Langston Hughes

You slung your poems over your shoulder
And bobtailed off, while the rubbed coins swirled
Through the subway slot. We rushed after,
called from the platform. Too late!
One palm slightly raised, you wavered
Down the shuddering aisle. You became a blur
adrift in a thousand tilting rooms.
No one had time to say goodbye.

We kept on, chewing our chicken,
picking our teeth, even as we flinched,
feeling the neon sharpen through the glass,
the shadows heavy on our bones.
But somewhere behind the counter
your laugh flickers. On a broken cup
you tap out a beat to make us dance.

But Anyhow

for Frank Smith   1932-1999

Frank leans over his keyboard,
with handfuls of notes
and the hunch of his back,
tells us what the blues are all about.
The words he lays down
matter less than how he turns them over
in his mouth. Between sets,
hearing about somebody else's pain,
he says it again—
Most nights he's up four, five times,
tunes lurching through his head.
Lugging the keyboard out to his van,
he mutters about how the body withers,
slides the door shut and says,
"But anyhow, you got to really swing."

Who?

Who lingers always when the dream has blanched?
Whose off beat mutters know the basest flesh?
Whose wails are joy in the silence of the heart?
Who blows the hottest vibraharp of all?
Who swings spirals of song 'round even the bird?
Who is the source of soul?
                    ADONAI

The Fiddle Found Jazz

for Stéphane Grappelli
and Claude Williams

Who could figure
the fiddle could do
what it does
when they're talking
like they do?

This line of players
like a wave of notes
appears and disappears
in the always-changing sky.
Whatever the weather they're there.
Their jazz lurks in the fiddle;
so does the music that feeds the jazz.
Whoever can find it will:
the Gypsy in his momentary place,
the mordant Jew crying out in Klezmer,
all those violinists in the pit,
all their bows pointing to Grappelli,
swinging between the stars.

After Blowing All Night

They been blowing all night
and now they're talking,
which means less,
saying how the music
keeps you going
through the killer days,
how what comes out
of the horn's better
than anything on your plate,
anything out of a glass
or a needle, better
than anything except
maybe a woman
and that's short time
except a rare sometimes
and how chasing either
too hard can do you in
like that cat Antony or Bird
strangled on a riff.

For Herman Leonard, Photographer

at the Barbara Gillman Gallery

Cyrano dueled, he said,
with his mind not his heart.
Michaelangelo revealed
what was already there.
Bechet practiced, he said,
'til he could think with his horn.

So how did Herman Leonard
find what he found?

One player tilts his trumpet up,
Conjuring music. Another face
half-smiles in concentration.
This singer is a hyacinth profile,
delicate as those currents
of change that swirl by
in a sea of jazz.
I think of Etheridge, too,
and his prison poems, his ultimate blues,
of how he made the wall of the joint
a shrine. Etheridge, your words,
swim through these pictures, in
and out of the light. God blesses
the artist for all his indirections

Here, in this silent gallery I listen
to notes ricocheting
into my heart. Etheridge is singing,
Fuck you, Pain, Freedom flies.
How does one find what one looks for?
What's under a porkpie hat?
Who's at the edge of the crowd
or inside the moment,
recognized and caught?
The photographer is nowhere
but always present,
and the music envelops us
like smoke or light,
and Bird and Dizzy, Miles,
Hot Lips and Etheridge Knight
keep right on playing
so we'll know we are alive.

Photo (left to right): Billy Bauer, guitarist.
Eddie Safranski, bassist. Charlie Parker,
alto, tenor saxophonist, and composer.
Lennie Tristano, pianist. New York City,
1949.

Photo © by Herman Leonard.

III   them blues

Breakdown Blues

When she said *goodnight* at last I knew
her *goodnight* really meant goodbye.
There wasn't much for me to do
but drive away and justify.

There wasn't time for me to spend
chasing her from tree to tree.
There comes a time when end means end,
and we break down to her and me.

It Sure is Risky

It sure is risky
when it comes to love.
One minute the two of you
are a ball of heat, the next
you're drinking cold coffee by yourself.
I haven't met one I can predict,
not one man, faithful or not.
Whether he stays or leaves
the fridge is empty at least half the time
and you end up with the blues.
It sure is risky
when you come to love,
but it's better than
never or *nowhere* or *notime* or *nothing*.
The blues is better than being without.

Too Late Blues

She told me love was somehow
always out of reach.
I said, "Baby, don't admit it's true."
She said she was sick to learn,
but there was no one round to teach.
Love was always somehow
out of reach.

I stretched across the table,
Put my fingers on her brow.
She stroked my arm and said,
"Too late now."
Love is somehow out of reach.

She's just inches from my hand
and light years from my heart.
She's drifting out in space;
we're galaxies apart.

I'm like a tired whale
stranded on a beach,
and love, love is, somehow,
out of reach.

With Women It's a Power Thing

With women it's called waiting.
First you wait to see if she was listening
when you played "Satin Doll,"
then to see if she meant that smile for you,
then what it was she meant—
and if it went deeper than you thought.
You wait to find out how long you must,
to learn if she is willing
to learn if surfaces mean anything
at all. Soon you're waiting
for what once you took for granted,
something no woman can accept.
So while you wait she changes
to something you're not sure you meant to wait for.
Before you know it, consider *that* expression,
you're waiting to learn the meaning of your life.

Honey Takes Off

I couldn't take those little things
they told me shouldn't matter,
the way he said I was "off key"
or couldn't tell "a player from a joke,"
all those sly male musician innuendoes,
like, "She sings the blues
with his money in her mouth."
You know the kind.
Come down to it, we
couldn't do it to each other
any more, so it was time
to let him do it to himself.

If This Were Eden

The bird that nested in the small of my spine
Turned into your hand. I was not stone.
A tiny wind poured into my ear
As if from a shell; it was your breath.

The butterfly that fluttered at my throat
Became your mouth. We are both alive
To the simple stars
By which the worlds are lighted.

If this were Eden and we loved,
I'd turn at the signal of your finger's touch.
I'd tremble like a pool brushed by a bough
When your leafy hand rippled my thighs.

Oh, if this were Eden and we loved,
We'd graft our sinews to our sense,
Make of breathing a honeyed flow,
Of flesh, the language of the wise.

Gravedigger Blues

The stock market suddenly falls.
You can't even beg a dime.
You make three hundred calls.
No one will give you the time.
Don't ask yourself why.
Don't bother to cry.
Be happy you come this far.

You can plot and plunder,
complain you ain't got everything.
While you're scheming, Baby,
autumn's catching up with spring.

When you come this far be happy,
Don't bother counting to ten.
Remember how you come this far.
You may not get the chance again.

Walking with Mingus

damn voices
sizzling through cracks

lemon rinds scattered
along curbs

    a lurching
      three-footed mutt,

    oil oozing from under
      an ancient olds.

damn city
    slum and civilization
            gone to rust

        the Breakdown
        the rupture of reason

        the flickering
        crosshairs of disease

          the damp holds

          the dirty lies
          that derange

          the snapping
          of tiny bones

and damn
the infants squalling
for mothers long lost
fathers mauled in smoke and fog

                    chain-link fences
                    strung out
                    along the checkpoints,

                            the scratching
                            for antique crockery
                            at the base of monuments

the pouring over signatures
over unsigned messages,

                      the pain
                          that sucks
                              at the root
                                  of the spine

                and damn

            this dreary bleating
            that makes us come
            undone
            in the daylong dark

Somewhere
they say
sunlight streaks
across a random leaf,

and one
             drop
                 of rain

                                 swings

                                                 from the edge of a bowl
                 like a note

             maybe

                 damn it

                                 damn it all

Ad Lib for the Frank Smith Trio

I spend the night
phoning old friends,
waking the years.
Who? they say
What? this is
insomnia calling I say,
I will not
let our connections
slip into death
fade across the miles
yes but not lost.
I call to remind you.

Waiting for the Music

Days like this, I swear I've lost my mind;
where, I don't know.
Like a lost noise, I drift through silence
till something stops me:
Langston's syncopated words,
jazz or wind on water.
They stir my feelings
till sweet imagination soars.
"Evolve, Baby," I tell myself,
And Langston answers, "Yah, Be-Bach."

Blues for Bernice Six

in tornado country
the neighbor down the road
can speak expert as Job
about the whirlwind,
how it can suck up all the years
and leave you standing
in your weathered boots
while someone you love
floats off like notes
into the busy air.
you pray her to the softest landing
knowing how grief can make
even the smallest town in Missouri
the center of the world.

Blues in Greek

My whole life is blue,
sometimes sky, sometimes sea,
crying sometimes
for you and me.

I heard a woman
sing the blues in Greek.
I can relate:
All that bright blue sea
in all that fate.

All Cats Turn Gray When the Sun Goes Down

The cat who glitters all around the town,
The up-tight cat who can't make a sound,
The cat who knows his way around,
They all turn gray when the sun goes down.

The swingin cat who's never been unwound,
The cat who whirls round and round and round,
The desperate cat who can't be found,
They all turn gray when the sun goes down.

Purple cat, yellow cat, pink or brown,
Ruffles or Killer or Old Tarreytown,
They all turn gray, Yah, they all turn gray,
They all turn gray when the sun goes down.

The fashion cat poured in her sequined gown,
The harried cat treed by a hound,
The cat who dreams of being crowned,
They all turn gray when the sun goes down.
They all turn gray when the sun goes down.

IV   ritmo Latino

Café con Leche

I'm drinking café con leche
at a Latin café on Lincoln Road.
Behind me a Cuban disc jockey
proclaims "Something Extraordinary!"
is about to play. The rhythms
are up like the south Florida sun.
I wish I could understand
more than the lingo, more
than the romance of corazon;
something about the heart's beat
under the languor that isn't calm
at all. Sitting here
I become aware
of the barest breeze, sure
not to provoke the humidity
with movement. What moves is inner,
the percussive drive
of Chucho Valdes or Machito,
even as I sip and linger.
A sudden flush of birds between the palms,
a strolling model reflected in a window,
a delivery man whose journeys
stitch the world together—
I'm right they say to contemplate
the rhythms in my mind,
to savor the stillness,
to let my heart keep time.

They're Playing "Bolero of the Cats" at GoJazz

Gato's stretching under a hibiscus,
Unlimbering in half-time
at the edge of the parking lot.
Inside GoJazz they're playing
Bolero of the Cats, Gato's favorite tune.
Who knows how he got here,
from which life he rose or descended.
Satch said, "Never look back,
you don't know who's following."
Here you never know
who'll sidle up
in what language
or who can really swing.
Some flutist from Caracas
is scatting on the bandstand now,
and the cats are all swinging
in a new time. Gato's gone
somewhere into the shadows,
purring in Portuguese,
ready to reappear
in a corner
under a portrait of Bird.

Rubalcaba in Montreal

Outside the club they shrieked
Gonzalo was a communist,
not a jazzman, a traitor.
He shouldn't play, they howled.
The rage of exiles in Miami
stunned him into silence.

Thousands of miles from home
we see him in a cool hall
of a northern country,
a dark Cubano in black garb, erect
behind a baby grand.

A hot/cold rush of notes
splashes our temples,
a piano-sax dialogue,
transfusion of Bach
and Santeria, Havana
and Montreal, births
quicker than daggers,
glittering as sunrise.

Walking back to our tourist hotel
We are outside language:
Francais, Español, or English.
Rubalcaba's in our heads,
his chords ensnaring our silence,
his rhythms between our footfalls.

Playing the Cajon

for Ira Sullivan, flute
and Oscar Salas, cajon

No matter.   No matter.
Whatever.   No matter.
The rumble, no matter.
The clatter, no matter.
What matters, the hand on the box,
the finger , the flutter,
whenever, however, the sound of the drum.
Remember the sound of cajon. It matters,
however the fingers will slide
or will flutter, always it matters:
the voice deep within
the box on which crouches
the drummer. He knows
how to reach for the heart
of the sound, with the roll
of his palm or the thump
of his thumb, no matter.
Whenever, no matter,
however, the sound
of forever's the sound
of cajon. From the side,
from the front, from the back
of the box, he coaxes the echoes,
the rumbles cajon
from deep within Cuba
has kept stored for so long.

One by one, falling,
notes filter like leaves
or the fleet wings of birds
out of the branches.
They mingle with echoes
that rise from cajon.
This flutist can spin
from the land of wild onions
a trail of bright notes.
They whirl 'round the drummer
who leans toward the ground
as he listens to echoes
that matter   that matter:
no matter how long
whenever   however
the flute and cajon,
the air through the flute,
the air in the drum,
what matters will matter,
the hands on the box, arpeggios
swooping in arcs through the trees,
what slides and what flutters,
what coaxes and echoes,
whenever however
the sound of cajon.

V   **bopping with Bird**

"Come, fill the cup, and in the fire of spring
your winter garment of repentence fling:
The Bird of Time has but a little way
to flutter – and the Bird is on the wing."

The Ruba'iy'at of Omar Khayy'am

Max

you are the world's greatest

Bird **Monk**

you are so sweet and beautiful

Monk **Dizzy**

my cup is overflowing listening to you all

Dizzy

I dig this atomosphere

Bird

well then how much you give me on my face?

Monk

make that a twelve bar line & we will all be rich

Bird

r u n s

monk deep

Dizzy **Max**

I feel like a two headed cat in a fish market

Max

hang on to your horns; we are about to become Airborne

67

Yardbird

In the alley
alongside
or out back
behind the dumpster
or in the gravel pit
next to the window well
he keeps peckin'
driving his beak
at the hardstuff
of the world
when you can't hear
he's behind the shed
out of range
or teaching worms
how to crawl
practicing
some low tune
later you'll hear
what you can't
even then you
won't know quite
what Yardbird's done.

Addie Parker's Blues

I be here waiting
When my boy drags home.
He know where to find me
When he feeling like a stone.

Whose back room you shacked up in,
High on the sound of your horn?
What gal's wailing "Baby,
Baby, for you I was born!?"

What game you playing, Baby,
Your Daddy didn't play?
Don't go balling with pretty Miss Bones
Or she roll you right away.

I hear them sirens crying down Troost,
Mr. Wheeler scuttling down the hall.
Woman, I asks myself, Woman,
Will your boy come home at all?

What game you playing, Baby,
Your Daddy didn't play?
Don't go balling with pretty Miss Bones
Or she roll you right away.

I be here waiting
When my boy drags home.
He know where to find me
When he feeling like a stone.

Up There

This one Bird makes such music
you're Dizzy in the leaves.
He can knock you off your limb,
straight or crooked, unless
you're ready for Bach
in a new time, in black feathers,
ready for wild chords
in intricate flights.
This is holy company
meant for contemplation,
for a Monk's devotion,
for the sky's applause.

Bird Meditation

Dr. told me something profound.
He said, Bird, you can't
mess up your body forever.
You're stuck in that sack of bones,
and it will tell you when
it won't carry you round no more.
I said, Dr. of Medicine, learned you may be,
I'm gonna beat the destiny you're bound to.
I'm gonna fly out of here with my soul together.

Cat asks me, Bird, then why you keep on taking the stuff?

I go to this heart specialist, you know,
give him a hundred dollars for heart relief.
He treats me. Don't do no good.
My heart's still messed up.
I go to this ulcer man,
give him 75 dollars to cool my ulcer out.
Don't do no good.
Meet this little cat in a dark alley around the corner.
I give him five dollars for a bag of shit;
my ulcer's gone, my heart trouble gone
all of my ailments gone.
Only got my life to worry about.

Doris Says Goodbye

I never said goodbye.
He wouldn't let me.
He is the sweetest talking man
when he wants to be. Sure
I love him still,
but I can't take it no more.
This way I'll live a while.
Charlie thinks you just go on and on,
that you always recover, no matter.
If your feet hurt, you take your shoes off.
If your heart hurts, you play.
He chews the moments up faster than french fries.
I just can't keep up. Who else can play so fast?
Oh, Bird, if you could only mellow out,
live life slow as a picnic Sunday,
we would have a long holiday. But you panic
the first boring second. You got to go,
hunting meaning or something,
got to drag somebody into something new,
got to break some notion down.
You are a hard man to stay with.
It's like keeping up with the running tide.
I just got to lie back on the beach awhile.
We had those good times, for sure.
I can always hear you if I close my eyes.

Bird Talks After Bellevue

In the vernacular of the streets, I flipped
when I heard Stravinsky's *Firebird*.
I dig what the doctors never hear.
All I need, even hung up
is someone playing,
tapping that foot.

Sometimes I get an idea
and try it. When I look at my fingers,
I'm surprised it's me.

That Bartok cat sends me far out.
Man, I dig, all the moderns.
Music. It's my experience, my thoughts.
If you don't live it, it won't come out
of your horn. They teach you
there's boundary lines.
But not to art, Man.
Notes come out of my pores.

Down at the Phoenix

Down at the Phoenix
notes flit through the rainbow.
They're playing "Ornithology"
in January, and nobody knows it's winter.
Before our eyes birds fly
out of the sax's mouth, synesthetic transformations
we can believe. It's still Charlie Parker's town,
his energy from another realm,
his lingo like a Sanskrit incantation
that remakes the world moment by moment.

Unveiling the Bird,
Lincoln Cemetery, Kansas City, Missouri

Of the poor who climbed to power
who can name the heroes?

In the unfashionable graveyard
between two cities,
they remark a plot
long overgrown.
Even the mayor's there,
and a vice-president of the local
greeting card company.
A dozen others, too,
out of a world
scrawled once with
BIRD LIVES!

Some found proof
in sudden swoops through windows,
jazz droppings peppering the establishment.
But now the Bird's caged
in wrought iron, framed
for his worshipers
like a sacred relic.

His notes spin off through the air
Like late November leaves.
But everyone's too down to notice,
even the hip black horn-blowing
sky pilot who thanks the Lord
for such an aviary.

This is a late unscrambling
of the dead, of mother
and son tangled in weeds,
while the greats, Max Roach
& Milt Jackson, weep
through the chilled air.

After Midnight

Last night the years surrounded me,
some bright as silver keys,
some like chords flickering in a dream.
The radio I slept by muttered jazz.
My clock glowed across the room,
its hands sweeping the seconds by,
the hours under,
the wind across the world.
Then Bird blew in,
blew back the clouds
that rained just yesterday,
and I heard that music of the spheres
the ancients heard.
I heard them blues
blown through a horn of stars.

Coda for a Horn Player

All you can do
Is what the Bird tried to:

Blow it out your soul
And hear it float back.

Let's play one for them.

Abel, Milt. Kansas City bassist and singer. Known for his rolling, compassionate style, Abel's rendition of the tune "Big Noise" is remarkable. Hear *Warm*.

Ahmad. Ahmad Jamal. Pianist. Known for his lean, spacious style, Jamal influenced many, including Miles Davis. Hear *Ahmad Jamal at the Pershing* (1958, Argo 628).

Basie. Count Basie (1904-1984). Pianist and bandleader. In Kansas City during the 1920s-30s, Basie moved from the Blue Devils to Bennie Moten's band, shared in organization of the Barons of Rhythm, and then started his own band, the legendary Count Basie Orchestra. Hear *One o'Clock Jump* (1937, Decca 1363), *April in Paris* (1955-6, Verve 8012).

Bechet. Sidney Bechet (1897-1959). Clarinetist and soprano saxophonist. Bechet, a consummate jazz soloist in the New Orleans style, popularized the soprano saxophone, influencing many, including Johnny Hodges and Buster Bailey. Few would even touch the soprano sax in challenge to Bechet, until Coltrane renewed its popularity in the 1960s. Hear *Sweetie Dear/Maple Leaf Rag* (1932, Vic. 23360).

Bird. Charlie "Yardbird" Parker (1920-1955). Alto saxophonist. Perhaps the most influential improvisatory soloist in jazz, a bop genius and virtuoso. Parker, born in Kansas, later moved to New York, where he worked with Gillespie and led his own quintet, composed of Davis, Jordan, Potter, and Roach (1947). Hear *Billie's Bounce/Now's the Time* (1945, Savoy 573), *Ornithology/A Night in Tunisia* (1946, Savoy 1002).

Dizzy or Diz. Dizzy Gillespie (1917-1993). Trumpeter, composer, and bandleader. One of the originators of the bop style in the early 1940s, Gillespie's style on trumpet is still widely imitated. He played fast, and he played lucidly. Hear *Salt Peanuts/Hot House* (1945, Guild 1003).

Doris. Doris Parker. Charlie Parker's wife. See Bird

Emily. Emily Dickinson (1830-1886). Poet. One of the most revered and influential American poets. See "Hope" Is the Thing with Feathers, I Heard a Fly Buzz--when I Died--, Success Is Counted Sweetest.

George. George Salisbury (1918-1986). Kansas City pianist and teacher. Much admired for his piano virtuosity.

Gonzalo. Gonzalo Rubalcaba. Cuban jazz pianist. A prodigy.

Grappelli, Stéphane (1908-1997). French violinist. Pioneer of the jazz violin, an improvisatory force. Hear *Violin Summit* (1966, Saba 15099).

Herb Six. Kansas City pianist (1909-2001). A melodic player, known for his beautiful chord changes, Herb Six also was a seminal jazz educator. As Prof. John Leisenring put it, "I consider Herb Six one of the fathers of the jazz education movement at UMKC." Herb Six helped put jazz in the conservatory. Composer of *All Cats Turn Gray When the Sun Goes Down*.

Hotlips. Hotlips Page (1908-1954). Trumpeter, singer. Page accompanied Bessie Smith and Ma Rainey, played in Bennie Moten's band in Kansas City, played briefly as principal soloist for the Count Basie band, played in Artie Shaw's band. Led his own bands, thrived on jam sessions. Hear *St. James Infirmary* (1947, Har. 1069).

Huggins, L. C. "Speedy" (1913-1999). Kansas City singer, tap dancer. Hear *The Scamps*.

Jackson, Milt. Vibraphonist, member of the Modern Jazz Quartet. A master improvisationalist, Jackson was one of the first vibraphonists to excel at bop. Hear *Bags' Groove* (1952, BN 1593).

Knight, Etheridge (1931-1991). Poet. Won the American Book Award. Discovered by Gwendolyn Brooks.

Lady, or Lady Day. Billie Holiday (1915-1959). Singer. Holiday, known for her light, rhythmic style, became one of the most popular jazz singers of her day. Her haunting ballads became standards. Her popularity continues. Hear Strange Fruit/Fine and Mellow (1939, Com. 526).

Langston. Langston Hughes (1902-1967). Poet. Champion of the Harlem Renaissance, Hughes documented the troubles of African Americans and musicians. Hughes drew upon the meters and moods of jazz and blues, echoing the stylistic progression of African American music with his verse. See "Montage of a Dream Deferred."

Marian. Marian McPartland. Pianist. Known for her elegant style, multifaceted technique. Hear her nationally syndicated radio program *Piano Jazz*.

Mary Lou. Mary Lou Williams (1910-1981). Pianist and composer. In the 1930s, Williams brought Andy Kirk's band to fame with her striking arrangements, compositions, and solos on piano. After Kirk's band, she led her own groups. Hear *Waltz Boogie* (1946, Vic. 202025), *Walkin' and Swingin'* (1936, Decca 809).

Max. Max Roach. Drummer, composer. Many of Roach's melodic riffs are now standards. Roach also helped move the pulse of the drum set from the bass drum to ride cymbal. Hear *Study in Brown* (1955, EmA 36037).

McShann. Jay McShann. Pianist. McShann, known for his percussive, nearly boogie-woogie style. One of Kansas City's piano legends. He first hired Parker, and he also hired Claude "Fiddler" Williams for his groups. Hear *Swingmatism/Vine Street Boogie* (1941, Decca 8570).

Mingus. Charles Mingus (1922-1979). Bassist, composer, bandleader. Known compositionally for his avant-garde montages of seemingly disparate styles. A technical and stylistic master on the bass, Mingus continues to influence generations of bassists and composers. Hear *Mingus, Mingus, Mingus, Mingus, Mingus* (1963, Imp. 35).

Monk. Thelonious Monk (1917-82). Bop and avant garde pianist and composer, known for his meditative, witty musical innovations. Legend has it Monk "invented" several piano voicings by making geometrical shapes with his hands, playing them on the keys, then accustoming himself to these new sounds. Hear *Brilliant Corners* (1956, Riv. 226); *Straight, No Chaser* (1966-67, Col. CS9451).

Parker, Addie. Charlie "Bird" Parker's mother.

Percy Bysshe. Percy Bysshe Shelley, "Adonai" (1792-1822). Romantic poet. Shelley worked in elaborate, elegant stanza forms and employed a complex tone, ranging from passionate to desperate, and dignified to urbane. His wife, Mary Shelley, wrote *Frankenstein*. See "Ozymandias," "Mont Blanc," "Ode to the West Wind."

Rollins, Sonny. Tenor saxophonist. Known for his colossal bop improvisations, often filled with "stream of consciousness," athematic responses to the tune's melody, Rollins is an on-the-spot composer/player rivaled perhaps only by Parker. Hear *Saxophone Colossus* (1956, Prst. 7079).

Rushing, Jimmy (1903-1972). Kansas City blues singer.

Salas, Oscar. All-star Latin drummer.

Satch. Louis Armstrong (1901-1971). Trumpeter and singer. A lively virtuoso trumpet soloist and singer, Armstrong heavily influenced the course of jazz through his improvisatory genius. He also led many legendary groups, including his Hot Five and Hot Seven. Hear *West End Blues* (1928, OK 8597), Bessie Smith: *St. Louis Blues* (1925, Col. 14064D). See Ken Burns' video series *Jazz*.

Sinatra, Frank (1915-1998). Singer. Hear *Frank Sinatra/Count Basie at the Sands* (1966, Rep. 1019).

Smith, Frank (1932-1999). Kansas City pianist. Known for playing remarkably strong, full phrasings. Hear *Frank Smith: From Kansas City to Tokyo* (JCCC).

Sullivan, Ira. Trumpeter and saxophonist. Master of the bop style--and many instruments. Formed a quintet with Red Rodney. Hear *Ira Sullivan Does It All* (1981, Muse 5242).

Verweire, Albert. Kansas City jazz musician.

Walt. Walt Whitman (1819-1892). Poet. A key 19-century American poet. See *Leaves of Grass*.

Whitmer, Tim. Kansas City pianist, protege of George Salisbury. Hear him at the Phoenix in Kansas City.

Williams, Claude "Fiddler." Kansas City fiddler and singer. Known for his lively, 1920s-30s style, Williams continues to influence younger musicians in Kansas City, most of whom can not keep up with him. Hear *Claude Williams: King of Kansas City* (1997, PCD 7100).

See also *The New Grove Dictionary of Jazz*, edited by Barry Kernfeld.

DAN JAFFE has written more than a dozen books. His jazz opera, *All Cats Turn Gray When the Sun Goes Down* (with Herb Six) has been produced in Kansas City, St. Louis, and New York. He also appears on the CD *In Their Own Voices: A Century of Recorded Poetry* (Rhino Records). Jaffe has performed his poetry with numerous jazz musicians, including George Salisbury, Milt Abel, Nicole Yarling, Frank Smith, Brian Murphy and Tim Whitmer. He currently lives in Miami Beach, Florida.

HERMAN LEONARD has been called "the world's greatest jazz photographer." The Smithsonian institution has collected his images of Charlie Parker, Louis Armstrong, Miles Davis, Duke Ellington, Count Basie, Billie Holliday, Sarah Vaughn, et al. Exhibitions of his work have appeared throughout the world. He now lives in New Orleans, Louisiana.